HOW TO STAY POSITIVE AND LIVE A STRESS-FREE LIFE

Simple Practice Of Living A Healthy And Happy Lifestyle By Overcoming the Storms

Copyright

ISBN: 978-1-7396635-3-7 (paperback)

MEET THE AUTHOR

Nijel James is a writer and author, and life model coach. The author of "THE SECRETS TO HAPPY PARENTING, HAPPY KIDS.

Understanding How Different Styles Affect The Development Of Your Kids."

Nijel James is passionate about humanity, and his goal is to impact lives by ensuring we all live happy life and achieve our purpose on earth.

Originally from the United Kingdom, he now lives in Asia.

We are in charge of our happiness, and this is the time to live it to the fullest.

DISCLAIMER

All knowledge contained in this book is given for informational and educational purposes only. The author is not accountable for any results or outcomes that emanate from using this material. Constructive attempts have been made to provide both accurate and effective information, but the author is not bound for the accuracy or use/misuse of this information.

INTRODUCTION

We all desire happiness. However, we often consider happiness something that happens to us and over which we have little influence. Our cerebrums have been created to assist us with getting by, safeguard ourselves, and remain safe. , As a result, we as a whole have cheerful minutes and times of joy and happiness. A significant number of us, then again, are pained by ongoing pessimistic feelings and are simply trapped in a "funk." kSatisfying your partner should be basics and shouldn't be a big deal. "If things were unique by some stroke of good luck, I'd be blissful," we could persuade ourselves.

Be that as it may, it isn't how satisfaction works. According to research, just 10% are not entirely settled by one's conditions. So, all in all, where does most of our happiness come from?

Character assumes a part in satisfaction. Certain individuals are brought into the world with a wonderful attitude. We, as a whole, know individuals who are, by and large playful and energetic. Their lively characters simplify satisfaction for them.

So, what does this mean for folks born with a cranky personality? They may focus on the negative aspects of individuals and circumstances rather than the positive aspects. As a result, their mood may be gloomy more often than happy. However, it is achievable if they want to be happier (and who wouldn't?).

Our thinking, the behaviors we adopt, and how we live each day affect how happy we are. We can use the key happiness factors to make ourselves happier by learning about them.

In this book, you will learn the simple practice of living a healthy and happy lifestyle by overcoming the storms. In addition, the book provides you with things you can do to make you live a happy and improved life, from cutting your worries, dealing with negativity, not allowing society to define you, looking beyond the dark side, and loving yourself to living your life with daily affirmations.

CHAPTER ONE

Discover How to Live a Happy Life

Happiness is more than a pleasant feeling or a cheerful expression. Being ready to make the most of your life is the feeling of fully appreciating it. We can achieve our best when we are happy.

Researchers discovered the following when studying cheerful people:

- Happy people are more successful
- Happy people are more likely to succeed
- Happy people are healthy
- People who are happy live longer
- Happy people have better connections
- Happy people learn better

What makes life more enjoyable for you? As with any other endeavor, building a long-term enjoyment takes discipline. We must, in a sense, reset our baseline. It won't happen immediately, but here are some things you can do every day to start learning the secrets of happiness:

Concentrate On The Positive

To attain long-term happiness, you must reprogram your brain from negative thinking to positive. Try the following: Look for the good in your life for one to two minutes. After 45 days of performing this three times daily, your brain will begin to do it automatically.

Pick a positive affirmation to rehash to yourself over the day, for example, "Today is delightful" or "I'm appreciative for all I have." Then, when things turn out badly, attempt to see what is happening with an inspirational outlook. But, again, remember the benefit of seeing the splendid side of things.

Perceive Small Victories

Numerous little triumphs go in the middle between the promising and less promising lifetimes. Pause for a minute to appreciate these humble triumphs.

Have you finished every one of the undertakings on your daily agenda that you've been putting off? Yippee! Did you at long last dispose of the thousand messages stacking up in your inbox? Woohoo! Appreciate these little triumphs. Everything adds up!

Figure Out Some Kind Of Harmony

Work consumes quite a bit within recent memory; however, it ought not to be our only movement. It's basic to seek after leisure activities and interests beyond work. Do you have a hobby? Is it safe to say that you invest energy with your friends, family, and companions? Do you work out consistently? Balancing your life will limit pressure and give you extra channels for articulation and delight.

Practice Mindfulness

By focusing on your cognizance and the current second, care reflection works. It's about not condemning and tolerating your sentiments. Care is characterized as being available, mindful, and asking. Tolerating our conditions diminishes pressure and permits us to see things for what they are. We can track down quiet and certification in ourselves by rehearsing care.

Be Inventive

Specialists have gained notoriety for being surly and miserable. In any case, research proposes that partaking in imaginative pursuits makes you more joyful. The people who invest energy practicing their creative mind and innovativeness are bound to be energetic and have opinions of long-haul bliss and prosperity. Composing, painting, drawing, and melodic execution are instances of innovative action.

Acknowledge Your Flaws

Many of us progress toward flawlessness and try to be our best selves. To be cheerful, however, you should acknowledge the flaws accompanying life. It is absurd to hold ourselves and other people to these norms since flawlessness is inconceivable. We will be left frustrated all of the time. Acknowledge that life is blemished and that that flaw has magnificence and beauty.

Do What You Like to Do

It's challenging to remain blissful, assuming that you disdain your work. Try not to squander your best for a long time on a task that you hate, regardless of whether it covers the bills. What are your obsessions? What are you excited about? Focus on laying out a work way that persuades you and furnishes you with an elevated degree of bliss. Your degree of bliss will rise decisively.

Make Meaningful Connections

Love, fellowship, and local area all remain closely connected with satisfaction. We want to draw in and interface with others as people. We intuitively look for our clan — individuals who will uphold, comprehend and show up for us as we explore life's high and low points. We feel forlorn and separated without certified connections. At the point when we seek joy with others, we are blissful.

Be You

Acting naturally is quite possibly the best method for expanding your bliss. That infers tolerating yourself for who you are instead of depending on others' acknowledgment. Find an opportunity to get to know yourself. What describes you? What are your qualities? On a deeper level, who are you? Search for ways of feeling quiet in your skin.

Give Back In-Kind

Give liberally of your time and money. Provide for the individuals who are out of luck. Provide for individuals you care about. Magnanimity and compassion are characteristics shared by the individuals who offer in return. Giving money to others has been connected to better well-being because it delivers a decent vibe that diminishes stress and puts a smile on one's face.

Spend Time Outdoors

Some scholars claim that today's ultra-connected generation is suffering from nature deficiency. But, according to studies, the more time we spend in nature, the more connected we are to the natural world around us and the happier we are. Our relationship with nature also helps us retain good mental health.

Reminisce Over Happy Times

Why do we adore everything vintage? Maybe it's because nostalgia brings us joy. Reminiscing about our past or nostalgic feelings can help us reconnect with feelings of love, wonder, and contentment. Our history molds and defines who we are. We can boost our self-esteem and feel more connected to others around us when we recall joyful memories.

Cutting Your Worries

Human beings are prone to worrying, doubting, or being concerned. A first date, a job interview, or an unpaid bill can cause worry. However, "natural" worry becomes excessive when unmanageable and continuous. Every day, you consider "what ifs" and worst-case scenarios. Anxious thoughts won't leave your head and interfere with your regular life.

Your emotional and physical health can be severely impacted by constant worrying, negative thinking, and expecting the worst. Having mood swings can drain your emotional reserves, make you jittery and restless, impede sleep and leave you headaches. It can make it difficult to focus at work or school. You may take out your frustrations on those closest to you, self-medicate with alcohol or drugs, or try to distract yourself by staring at a screen. Chronic worrying is also a symptom of Generalized Anxiety Condition (GAD), a prevalent anxiety disorder characterized by tension, nervousness, and a general sense of unease that permeates your entire life.

Here are ways to cut your worries:

Make A "Worry Period" For Yourself

Set aside a certain time and location for worrying. It should be the same daily (for example, in the living room from

4:00 to 4:20 p.m.). Then, during your concern phase, you are free to worry about anything on your mind.

Make A List Of Your Concerns

Write down anxious thoughts or dreads that come to your mind throughout the day. Then you can move on with your day. It will be time for you to consider it later, so don't worry about it right now. Furthermore, writing down your thoughts—on a pad, phone, or computer—is far more difficult than merely thinking about them, so your anxieties are more likely to fade away.

You may worry about the thoughts you wrote down if they still bother you during the worry period. Allow yourself to worry only as long as you have designated for this period. Examining your concerns will frequently make forming a more balanced viewpoint simpler. And if your troubles seem unimportant any longer, simply end your worry time and go about your day.

Defeat Anxious Thoughts

If you have chronic anxiety and concern, you may perceive the world as more dangerous than it is. For example, you might overestimate the likelihood of things going wrong, jump to worst-case scenarios right away, or treat every nervous thought as fact. You may also doubt your ability to deal with life's challenges, fearing that you'll crumble at the first hint of adversity.

Challenge your negative ideas by asking yourself the following questions throughout your concern period:

- What proof do you have that the thought is correct? That's not the case?
- Is there a more optimistic, realistic perspective on the situation?
- What are the chances that what I'm afraid about will happen? What are some more likely possibilities if the chance is low?
- Is the idea beneficial? What good will thinking about it do me, and what harm will it do me?
- What would I say to a buddy who was concerned about this?

Differentiate Between Solvable and Intractable Concerns

According to research, worrying makes you feel less worried for a short time. Running through the problem in your thoughts distracts you from your emotions and gives you the impression that you're accomplishing something. However, worrying and fixing problems are two completely different things.

Problem-solving entails assessing an issue, devising clear strategies to address it, and implementing the plan. Worrying, on the other hand, seldom results in a solution. You're no more equipped to deal with worst-case events, no matter how much time you spend thinking about them.

Is Your Concern Manageable?

Worries that are productive and solvable can be addressed straight away. For example, if you're concerned about your expenses, you could contact your creditors to inquire about flexible payment arrangements. Worries that are unproductive and insoluble have no corresponding action. "What if I develop cancer?" or "What if my child is involved in a car accident?"

Start brainstorming if the problem is solvable. Write down every possible solution. Focus less on finding the perfect solution. Consider changing what you can instead of focusing on events or facts that you cannot change. After you analyze your options, create an action plan. As soon as you begin to work on the problem, you'll feel less anxious.

Accept the uncertainty if the worry is unsolvable. Most of your worrying thoughts will fall into this category if you're a persistent worrier. Worrying is a common approach for us to forecast what the future holds in store, avoid unpleasant surprises, and control the outcome. The issue is that it does not work. It doesn't make life any more predictable to think about all the things that could go wrong. Focusing on the worst-case situations can prevent you from appreciating the nice things you have now. Face your need for clarity and instant answers to stop worrying.

- Do you tend to forecast terrible things because they are unpredictable? What are the chances that they will?

- Is it possible to live with the possibility of anything bad happening despite the low probability?
- Inquire your friends and relatives about how they deal with uncertainty in different scenarios. Could you follow suit?

Pay attention to your feelings. However, by tuning into your sensations, you can begin to embrace them, even if they are unpleasant or illogical.

Overcoming Your Worries And How To Live Your Passion

You must overcome your worries and live your life passionately when you have identified and cut your worries. You must:

Recognize And Observe Your Concerns

Do not try to ignore, battle, or control them as you would normally. Instead, merely observe them as if from afar, without responding or passing judgment.

Talk About Your Worries To Conquer Them

Talking face-to-face with a trusted friend or family member is an excellent way to calm your nervous system and reduce anxiety; someone who will hear you out without condemning or being constantly distracted. When your fears become overwhelming, talking things out can seem less dangerous.

Keeping your troubles to yourself will only make them grow until they become overpowering. However, stating them aloud can frequently help you understand and put things into perspective. If your anxieties are unfounded, expressing them can help you see them for what they are: unfounded concerns. If your anxieties are justified, talking about them with someone else can lead to solutions you wouldn't have thought of on your own.

Create A Solid Support System

Humans are highly sociable creatures. We were not designed to dwell in solitude. However, a strong support system does not always imply a large circle of friends. Don't discount the value of having a few individuals you can rely on to be there for you. It's never too late to make new friends if you don't feel like you have someone to confide in.

Get Rid Of Your Worries

When you don't control your nervous thoughts, they pass quickly, like clouds passing through the sky. You become stuck only when you engage your worries.

Keep your attention on the now. Pay attention to how your body feels, your breathing pattern, shifting emotions, and the things that pass through your head. To move forward, you must get your attention back to the moment.

Repeat Everyday

It's a basic concept to utilize mindfulness to stay in the present moment. Even yet, reaping the advantages takes time and consistent practice. You'll probably discover that your thoughts constantly return to your anxieties at first. Avoid becoming frustrated. Keeping your focus on the present will help you break the negative worry cycle.

We all want to live passionate lives, yet getting there can be difficult. So read on to learn methods to start a life of passion if you want to wake up every morning inspired and ready to set the world on fire by doing what you love.

Make Yourself Visible

You must put yourself out there to live a life of passion. Volunteer for all possibilities that arise. Raise your hand if you want to try something new. Try something new. Putting oneself out there will offer a whole new universe of options and methods to live a passionate life daily.

Share Your Passion

Find folks who share your interests and get to know them. Surrounding yourself with passionate people about what they do will put you in an "everything is possible" mindset, making attaining your goals that much easier. "You are the sum of the five individuals closest to you," states an adage. So make sure you're around people pursuing their dreams, and you'll soon be one of them.

Incorporate Passion Into Your Everyday Life Piece By Piece

It doesn't have to be a one-size-fits-all strategy. Assuming that you're prepared to begin carrying on with life more energetically, you may begin right now by making little adjustments to your routine. Start living your energy in little ways right now, and then gradually increase the amount of what you value. With time, you'll be closer to continuing your fantasy life.

Understand Yourself

You must first learn to know yourself before you can begin. Learn what you enjoy doing, what gives you natural energy, and what drains and depletes you. Knowing yourself will help you determine whether your passion is the best fit.

Begin to Take Action

Nothing amazing has ever happened without major action! Start taking action right now to move closer to your goals. It may be as simple as conducting some online research, enrolling in an art class, or sending letters to local community groups about volunteering. Take the first step today, whatever it is.

Make Your Passion A Part Of Who You Are

To begin living a life of passion, you must first identify with it deeply. It's pointless to pursue things that are only superficially appealing, so be sure your passion is something that connects profoundly with you both inside and out first.

Prioritize Yourself

It's admirable to prioritize others, but there are times when you must prioritize yourself. Of course, supporting your family and being available to your friends is crucial. However, you may still create time for what's important in other aspects of your life by reducing your unneeded obligations. Make time in your weekly schedule to pursue your passions, and you'll get there eventually.

Take A Chance

Taking a risk is sometimes necessary to attain a goal. It might be as basic as making a new friend or as radical as quitting your day job. It's critical to consider the most extreme risks before taking them and ensure that you can make them work practically. There are moments when you just have to go for it. When the time is right, you'll know.

Maintain the momentum

Maintain your momentum by doing something that brings you closer to your life of passion. Because some days are busier than others, not every day will be a refuge for productivity and goal achievement. So do one thing every day to get closer to your goals, no matter how busy you are.

Have Faith In Your Abilities

You must believe in yourself above anything else. Nobody will believe in you if you don't believe in yourself; thus, it begins with you! Believe in the strength of your dreams, and know that even if the road doesn't belong to you, you'll make it

CHAPTER TWO

Dealing with Negative Thoughts

To deal with your negative thoughts, you've got to recognize them. Not sure whether your thought is constructive or destructive? Negative self-talk can take many forms, including:

Filtering

You emphasize the bad features of a situation while ignoring the favorable parts. For instance, you had a fantastic day at work. You completed your work ahead of schedule and were praised for your speed and thoroughness. But, unfortunately, you forget about the compliments you received that evening and concentrate solely on your plan to do even more homework.

Personalizing

You instantly blame yourself whenever something goes wrong. For example, if you learn that an evening out with friends has been canceled, you could conclude that no one wants to be around you.

Catastrophizing

You naturally prepare for the worst, even though the worst is unlikely to occur. For example, your order is incorrectly filled at the drive-through coffee shop; as your day continues, you're afraid it'll be a failure.

Accusing

Instead of taking responsibility for your actions, you try to blame someone else. You try to keep your ideas and feelings to yourself.

You "should" do something, you say. So you make a mental list of all the things you should be doing and then blame yourself for not doing them.

- **Magnifying:** You magnify minor issues.
- **Perfectionism:** Maintaining unattainable standards and striving for perfection is a recipe for disaster.
- **Polarizing:** Things are only good or awful to you. There is no such thing as a neutral position.

Having realized your negative thoughts, you have to get rid of them. To do so, positive thinking is emphasized. Positive thinking can be learned. Although the procedure is straightforward, it does necessitate time and practice because you are forming a new habit. Here are some suggestions for thinking and acting more optimistically:

Determine what needs to be changed

If you want to be more optimistic, start by identifying areas where you generally think negatively, such as your job, daily commute, life changes, or a relationship. Taking an aspect to improve on can be a good start. Instead of negative ideas, think of good ones to help you manage your stress.

Examine Yourself

Stop and think about what you're thinking at least once a day; if you notice that your thoughts are primarily negative, attempt to find a way to turn them around.

Allow Yourself To Laugh At Yourself

Is laughter the best medicine? Indeed, several studies have proven that laughter can heal both your body, your mind, you're your soul. Here are a few benefits of laughter:

- The first benefit of laughter is that it helps increase blood flow.
- Laughter prevents diseases. Studies have shown that laughter lowers blood pressure, releases muscle tension, decreases feel-good hormones, and burns calories.
- Laughter improves your emotional health.
- Laughter strengthens your spirit.

Now, allow yourself to smile or chuckle, especially when things are challenging. Look for humor in everyday events. You feel less anxious when you can laugh at yourself.

Maintain A Healthy Way of Living

On most days of the week, aim to exercise for 30 minutes. You can also do it in 5- or 10-minute increments throughout the day. Exercise has been shown to improve mood and reduce stress. To energize your mind and body, eat a healthy diet. Get plenty of rest. Also, master stress-reduction practices.

Make A Nice Environment For Yourself

Make sure the people in your life are encouraging and supportive and that you can count on them for sound advice and comments. Negative people might make you feel more stressed and doubt your capacity to manage stress healthily.

Self-talk should be positive. Begin with a single rule: Say nothing to yourself that you wouldn't say to another person. Treat yourself with kindness and optimism. If a negative thought arises, critically examine it and answer with affirmations of your positive qualities. Give thanks for the blessings in your life.

Do's and Don'ts

Here are some examples of do's and don'ts to apply a positive thinking twist to your thoughts:

Putting Positive Thinking Into Practice

Don't Say	Rather Say
I've never done it before.	It's an opportunity to learn something new.
I'm excessively lazy to finish this.	I was unable to squeeze it into my timetable; however, I can reevaluate a few needs.
It's too complicated.	I'll tackle it from a different angle.
I don't have the resources.	Necessity is the mother of invention.
There's no way it will work.	I can try to make it work.
No one bothers to communicate with me.	I'll see if I can open the channels of communication.
This may get a little worse for me.	I'm going to try a different approach.
It's too radical a change.	Let's take a chance.

You may not become a hopeful person in a short period if you usually have a negative outlook. With training, you'll find that your self-talk will contain less self-analysis and more self-acknowledgment. You also become less reproachful of your surroundings.

To cope with stress better, you must maintain a positive attitude. The health benefits of optimistic thinking may be related to that ability.

Not Allowing Society To Define You

Before breaking away from society's rules and standards, you must first comprehend and know yourself. Knowing oneself is inextricably linked to the goals you establish for yourself. Because understanding the significance of one's existence leads to understanding oneself, one must examine oneself as one who exists and lives.

It is up to you to determine the meaning of your life. You have the option of living a meaningless life or one with meaning. Your perspective will always determine the meaning of life; others may not share your viewpoint, but it has no bearing on how or what you define as your life's purpose.

As an individual who understands how to ponder, contemplate, and reflect on your own life, only you can provide meaning to it. Deep down, your entirety is demonstrated by definition. Recognizing, accepting, and understanding such a purpose is the key to becoming who you are.

Never forget to live life to the fullest and not let societal conventions and standards define who you are and will become. To become the joyful person you desire, you must live life without restrictions and strive for self-development.

- Do what you believe is right and be yourself. Your sort of person should never be dictated by society or your "following."
- It is acceptable to be ambitious and assertive if you are a woman.
- If you're a man, it's also okay to be quiet and passive. Society shouldn't define who you are. Those that succeed are those who defy customary norms.

We are so preoccupied with what others think of us that we forget about ourselves. That is, after all, what matters most.

Wallowing In Negative Thoughts

You may be locked in a negative mindset because you don't know what to do with your feelings or feel entitled.

Your first reaction after a traumatic event is loneliness, followed by a need to communicate with your loved ones. This is how humans are made. The deeper your unhappiness, the more you want to vent to your pals, and the longer it takes you to do it. People typically turn to drink, listen to melancholy music, and read sad novels when they are alone. Wallowing in gloomy ideas as a result.

However, the longer you retain a negative mindset, the more likely you will forget who you are. You lose sight of your goodness and continue to believe in your negative beliefs.

Accepting your feelings is associated with less brooding; however, wallowing in your emotions is not the same as dealing with them. This could be because brooding/wallowing necessitates investigating and evaluating one's sentiments. Acceptance helps to alleviate judgment. Accepting bad sentiments has no negative implications when it comes to happy emotions.

Accepting your feelings is not the same as accepting your circumstances: Acceptance of one's circumstances has two sides. Stopping yourself from striving against things you can't change can be useful, but it can also lead to passive resignation.

Accepting and enjoying one's emotions and ideas is an active process that comprises accepting and liking one's feelings without judgment.

Don't bury your feelings, but also don't dwell on them. When things get tough, and you're furious, frightened, depressed, or anything else, try to let it all out.

Learning To Walk Away

While some people may require professional assistance, there are easy measures you can take to help you break free from a negative mindset and develop more joy, vitality, and connection in your life.

Take A Breath And Think About It

Take a break if you're worried, apprehensive, or engaged in a negative thought habit. Instead, concentrate your five senses on the broad surroundings.

Recognize The Variation

Be aware of the difference between being stuck in your thoughts and enjoying the current moment through your five senses. Take note of your mental activities as well. Did you have an internal debate? Have trouble refuting critical or negative self-evaluations? Trying to get rid of unfavorable ideas or images? Examine whether or not this mental battle is beneficial to you.

Identify Your Thought

Sometimes, take a step back and label your thoughts as they are instead of literal truths. One example is slowing down your thoughts and adding the stem "I have the notion that..." to them. Continue categorizing without attempting to soften, change, or escape whatever thoughts you're thinking at the time. Consider how it feels to have some distance between you, the thinker, and your thoughts.

Select Your Thought

You'll be better able to choose your intention and the next correct move for you once you've paused from your mental fight, noticed what's happening and how it's been operating, and labeled your ideas for what they are—simple, temporary mental weather. Will you keep fighting your thoughts? You have the option of taking a little step toward something important to you. You'll see positive benefits as soon as you replace negative thoughts with positive ones.

CHAPTER THREE

Being Kind To Yourself and Not Be Hard On Oneself

You'll only ever have a relationship with one person: yourself. It takes kindness to acknowledge yourself as a friend.

Here are some methods to be kind to yourself while also being harsh:

Schedule Some Time Alone

Make time for yourself every day to do something enjoyable. You can sketch, journal, write short tales, play an instrument, or do whatever you choose. Allow yourself some "me time" to be kind to yourself each day.

Acknowledge Yourself

We're often quick to praise others' accomplishments but sluggish to recognize our own. This must come to an end. Acknowledge and reward yourself for your achievements.

Take a moment to think about something you're grateful for. Rejoice at your accomplishment. Compliment yourself. "Congratulations, me!" pat yourself on the back.

Develop Your Inner Activist

The inner critic is something we've all experienced. That small voice in our thoughts is quick to judge and always has a rebuke ready. Now is the time for your inner critic to meet your inner supporter.

And who is this inner advocate, exactly? It's a different voice in your head defending you. When your inner critic mocks and scorns you, your internal advocate intervenes and makes arguments on your behalf. Your inner critic is on your side, but your inner champion is on your side.

- Be kind to yourself by cultivating your inner advocate.
- Please Forgive Yourself

Everyone makes mistakes. Examine the following:

- ➤ Maybe you did something you're not proud of in the past.
- ➤ Perhaps you failed to defend yourself and let someone else take advantage of you.
- ➤ Because you were afraid, you may have missed out on a fantastic chance.
- ➤ Maybe you didn't complete a crucial task.

Stop criticizing yourself, promise to do better, and forgive yourself if you're furious at yourself.

Look After Yourself
34

Taking care of yourself is one of the most effective ways to show kindness. Get enough rest, eat plenty of fruits and vegetables, and exercise often. Additionally, find a means to relieve stress, keep yourself well-groomed, and take care of your appearance. Treat yourself if you see something you like. Save up for it if it's pricey. You don't have to wait for it to be given to you as a present.

Remind Yourself Of Your Positive Attributes

You may be a little overweight than the "ideal body type," but your hair is long and beautiful. You may not be a natural athlete, but you excel at math. You have a terrific sense of humor, even if you are theatrical. Always remind yourself of your positive characteristics.

Take a Step Forward

You have two options when you make a mistake, fail, or do something wrong. You can either break or build yourself up. Naturally, self-kind people prefer the latter.

Assure yourself that it will all turn out fine. First, remind yourself of your accomplishments in the Past to increase your morale. After that, devise a strategy for dealing with the situation and implement it.

Respect Your Dreams

People that appreciate and care for themselves honor their dreams. They don't dismiss their dreams as stupid delusions. Instead, they take their dreams seriously, turning them into objectives and devising a strategy for reaching them.

Find the Balance Between Acceptance and Effort

Recognize your potential as part of being kind to yourself. However, it is unfair to you to never be pleased with where you are or what you have accomplished thus far.

Accept your current state. You have your advantages and disadvantages. You succeed occasionally and fail occasionally. You're correct sometimes and incorrect other times. Allow yourself to be completely authentic.

Find a happy medium between being content with who you are and striving to improve.

Have Self-Belief

Desiring the best for oneself is a part of being kind to yourself. You should have confidence in yourself to accomplish the best outcomes. Believe in yourself and your ability. Believe in yourself and think positively about yourself.

Looking Beyond The Dark Side

Happiness should not be contingent on circumstances beyond one's control. You will be disappointed if you believe you will be happy only when you obtain something, become someone, travel somewhere, or meet someone. Not happiness, but pleasure.

Happiness does not imply perfection. Instead, it indicates that you have chosen to look past flaws. Yearning for perfection rather than accepting and loving yourself only holds you back. Joy is thwarted by resistance and desire for something different or more. Worse, it degrades contentment, preventing enjoyment.

Knowing who you are and your mission will help you move forward from your dark moment. Knowing what drives you is crucial to letting go of your bad moment and accepting yourself.

Be firm and own your role in something bigger. Create a life centered on ideals like service, love, and compassion.

CHAPTER FOUR

Managing Your Success

Accepting achievement can be just as difficult as accepting defeat. Some people are never satisfied with themselves. Here are a few ideas to help you retain and foster the capacity to be glad for yourself.

Believe In Yourself and Your Ability

Many people who have realized their dreams believe they did not deserve it. This can arise from various sources, and it's commonly referred to as the imposter syndrome in psychology.

Don't put yourself down. If it weren't for you, you wouldn't be where you are now. For example, let's say you don't think you give yourself enough credit. In that situation, it may lower your self-esteem, impairing your efforts to achieve achievement.

Celebrate Your Achievements

Ambitious folks skip the sushi supper and move on to the next task most of the time. You must celebrate your victories since they aid in integrating the success chip into your brain. You deserve it, after all.

Set Aside Yesterday

We've all failed, and anyone who says otherwise is lying. You can't be successful without making a few mistakes. Accept responsibility for previous mistakes and then move forward.

Don't Hold Your Breath for Tomorrow

Be glad for what you've achieved; however, don't go overboard with the idea that there will generally be a lift to the top. Every successful person experiences ups and downs. It's not always easy, but being pleased with where you are today is a rather simple attitude adjustment.

Accept Not Being Elon Musk

Do you genuinely want to be the world's richest person, or is your life already perfect, and you just want it to be nicer? Bill even decided to give away his billions to those in need because he does not require so much wealth to live a happy life. You don't, either.

Reward Those Who Helped You

Assume you're fortunate enough to have supportive friends and family. It's critical that people feel valued in that situation. People desire a pat on the back and be recognized by their peers and money.

Recognize That Success Can Alter How People Perceive You

Most successful people find that they are treated differently after achieving fame and money, and it isn't always for the better. Certain individuals might be jealous of your achievements. Monitoring your environmental factors and looking for free exhortation will help you in keeping away from individuals who might exploit you or attempt to take what you have.

- Accept And Nominate Yourself For Awards: Awards give you the confidence to think you have earned your accomplishment.
- Share Your Joy With Those You Care About One way or the other, without the love and support of your friends and family, and colleagues, you would not be where you're today. So try your hardest to express gratitude to everyone in your group. It makes you all feel better.

Does Money Give Happiness?

We've all heard the phrase "money can't buy happiness." However, we all spend money, and it is a limited resource for the most part. So how can we spend our hard-earned money in ways that bring us the most joy? Before you make your next purchase, consider what psychological research says about the relationship between money and happiness.

- **Being Wealthy Isn't Always A Guarantee Of Happiness**

Money is a major tool for one's happiness but doesn't define one's happiness. A larger salary, for example, can provide us with safer housing, better health care and nutrition, a more rewarding job, and more free time. This, however, only works up to a point. Once our fundamental needs for food, health care, safety, and housing are addressed, money's benefits—such as buying your ideal home—are frequently counterbalanced by the negative consequences of money—such as working longer hours or in more stressful occupations to preserve that income.

- **Doing Makes Us Happier Than Having**

Most individuals believe that "things" bring greater enjoyment than "experiences." Going to a concert or vacation lasts longer than physical items like the latest iPhone, handbag, or automobile. Purchasing goods makes us joyful, at least temporarily. But, in the long run, we become accustomed to new experiences. Even though they initially made us joyful and eager, the item soon becomes the new normal and fades into the background. Purchasing experiences, on the other hand, tend to make people happier over time. One explanation for this is that we frequently discuss our experiential purchases. It won't take long before you and your family reminisce about your Colorado trip. You'll even laugh at the time your car broke down, and you had to stay the night in a seedy motel.

- **Consider Spending Money On Others**

Many people accept that burning cash on themselves instead of others will make them more joyful. Notwithstanding, analysts have tried to analyze how satisfied people are after they have spent their yearly extra. They found that people are more joyful when they spend these extras on others or give it to a noble cause instead of on themselves. This happens no matter what the size of the reward. Therefore, providing for others helps us have a positive outlook on ourselves, as indicated by this reality.

Relationship Challenges and How to Compromise

It's an uncommon marriage where one doesn't encounter difficulties. You'll have a far greater chance of getting over relationship troubles if you can identify them ahead of time.

Every relationship goes through challenges, but those who have found success have learned to maneuver and maintain their relationships. Throughout life, they overcome challenges and complexities and learn how to cope.

Relationship difficulties include:

Communication

Unfortunate correspondence is the base of all relationship challenges. But, unfortunately, while taking a look at your BlackBerry, sitting in front of the TV, or flipping through the games segment, you can't impart.

Sex

Sex plays a major role in one's life, and it is important to understand each other sex life, how to satisfy each other and how to communicate with each other.

Feedbacks are important when it involves two people transacting; talk to your partner about her lapses and look for ways to improve.

What are the things he or she needs to do to get better or certain things you enjoy?

Cash

Indeed, even before the marital promises are traded, cash concerns can emerge. They can come about because of charming charges or the excessive expense of a wedding. So couples with cash issues ought to take a full breath and have a genuine conversation about funds.

Conflict

The struggle is an inescapable component of life. If, then again, you and your companion feel like you're living in a bad dream with similar terrible situations rehashing the same thing many days, now is the right time to be liberated from this poisonous propensity. You must understand there's no way a couple would live together and there won't be disagreement. It is, however, important to look for ways to put aside these issues and learn to resolve them before going to bed. Understand one another, and most importantly, learn to communicate, listen and apologize whenever you're wrong.

Trust

A relationship's foundation is trust. Do you notice anything that makes you doubt your partner? Do you have unresolved issues that make it difficult for you to trust others?

To save your relationship, you'll need to compromise. Unfortunately, compromise isn't always easy to achieve. You win a bit here and there. You lose a bit here and there. But what if neither of you is willing to make sacrifices in your relationship? In those circumstances, your relationship is likely to enter a stalemate. Here are ways you can compromise to save your relationship:

Take The Long View

Step back from the situation and consider whether or not this issue is important in the long run. Does it make a difference whether you ate Chinese or Thai for supper five years ago? It may be a different story if you utilize your savings to purchase a house or go on a dream vacation! Put your problem into perspective by using time as a lens.

Put On A Different Pair Of Shoes

Ask yourself honestly how you see the scenario from your partner's perspective. This is an opportunity to improve your emotional intelligence and empathy. What effect does it have on them? How does it feel from their perspective? The saying goes, never judge a man before you've walked a mile in his shoes. Looking at your problem from a different perspective could help you develop your solution.

Third Place Is The Winner

You don't have to pick first to win. In a relationship, you already have two options: yours and theirs. Are you able to locate the lovely third option? Compromise success is achieved by combining your demands and desires into a new version. Perhaps you will discover an entirely new choice; perhaps it will be a combination. What's important is that winning in a relationship isn't necessary for you coming in the first place. Winning is being content, and that might take some concession.

Exercise Your Body and Mind

Adaptability is vital. If you're not willing to bend your rules, you will face lots of challenges that might affect your relationship. As firmness carries a throbbing painfulness to your body, You need to be flexible in your relationship. Try to learn and unlearn certain things.

Suppose you aren't willing to change your position and stretch yourself with new challenges. In that case, you and your relationship will remain stagnant.

Compromise is much easier to achieve when you take a flexible approach.

CHAPTER FIVE

Putting Yourself First

The significance of putting oneself first should be taught in schools. It's a difficult talent to master, especially if you were up in a culture that glorifies putting others first. What's terrible is that, even in this day and age of social media, with so much knowledge about things like this, many people still struggle to put it into practice. That could be because not everyone understands the value of prioritizing one's needs. So, let's get started with it.

One of the first things to realize is that this does not imply becoming selfish. Selfish people are mostly concerned with themselves and have little regard for others. Putting yourself first typically entails considering your and others' needs and feelings. Nonetheless, you do what is best for you while avoiding harming others. And you must do so because, believe it or not, no one else will. It is entirely up to you to look after your physical and emotional well-being. You must create the life you choose. You must ask for what you require or desire because no one else will provide it for you.

Putting yourself first might feel frightening when you've been this person your whole life, especially if you've never done it before. However, this eventually leads to animosity. Some of the usual adverse effects include feeling underappreciated, undervalued, low self-esteem, burnout, and mental tiredness.

So, what does it mean to put yourself first? Here are some good habits to start with:

Establishing Limits

Setting limits may appear to be the most challenging aspect of prioritizing yourself. It appears frightening since we have no idea how the other person will react. It's human nature to be concerned about what others think of you. However, some people find it easy to express their boundaries, while others do not, and they must make that extra effort. People will continually cross you, push you to your limits, try your tolerance, and challenge your threshold if you don't do so, and you won't know how to handle it, leading to rage outbursts, breakdowns, etc.

Speaking Up When Necessary

Setting boundaries also has the effect of encouraging people to speak up. However, it also entails expressing your desires and emotions and requesting what you desire. Once you've mastered this, you'll nearly never settle for anything less than you deserve.

Setting Up a Healthy Routine

Taking care of your mental and physical health is important in prioritizing yourself. It's a crucial component. Establishing a personalized routine for your own needs will only help you grow into a happier person. Disrupting your daily routine for anything else simply implies you're not prioritizing your natural requirements. Even if you're not doing it because you're lazy, it demonstrates that you don't care. Cheat days are not permitted. Consider this.

Never Give Up

Setbacks are inevitable in life. Even if you put in your best effort, you may still fall flat on your face. This is especially true in entrepreneurship, where many new enterprises fail. You can find yourself in a situation where your brand cannot attract investors. Perhaps you didn't comprehend current workplace trends, and as a result, your organization suffered from high turnover.

Naturally, issues and difficulties can arise in your personal life. The challenges that come your way can feel overwhelming at times, whether dealing with personal finances or your romantic life. So, how do you deal with these depressing times? First, you rise to your feet. You don't give up on yourself just because others have done so. There are numerous compelling reasons to keep trying.

Every Issue Has A Solution

There is a saying that inventors invest 5% of their energy on the issue and 95% of their experience getting the solution. For example, Thomas Edison famously tried over 1,000 times to make an incandescent light bulb before achieving his goal.

Those Who Keep Trying are Rewarded by Life

A great deal of experimentation is expected on the way to progress. The plain truth is that large numbers of the world's best individuals were not honored with an ideal life. In any event, when life got them down, they were steady and continued to attempt.

When J.K. Rowling penned Harry Potter, she was a jobless single mother. Before becoming a Nobel Prize-winning physicist, Albert Einstein failed his university admission exam. Before becoming one of the most powerful presidents in the United States, Abraham Lincoln ran multiple unsuccessful electoral campaigns.

Each of these people had the option of giving up. But they persisted, and their perseverance paid off when they finally succeeded.

Other Resources For Assistance

It can be very demoralizing to be seen by others as a hopeless case. However, this does not mean you are utterly alone.

Even if you've explored all of the connections in your existing network, there may still be someone who can assist you. So you only need to be willing to explore outside your present network to find those who can help you, whether it's a support group to help you get through a personal difficulty or a new business link to help you revitalize your firm.

Professional networks and support groups can provide useful insight from others dealing with similar issues. Even online communities can provide valuable support and guidance. A new viewpoint from someone who isn't as close to you might sometimes provide the spark of insight you need to achieve your objectives. Even better, you might be able to assist someone else in the future.

Your Refusal To Surrender Might Influence Others

Not abandoning yourself won't just work on your life; it will likewise work on the existence of others. Your good thoughts can change an industry or help others work on their lives. You could try and act as an illustration to other people who can gain from your accomplishment and apply it to their battles.

Who knows what the world will pass up on the off chance that you surrender now. Many individuals who have changed the world could never have succeeded if they had surrendered after

51

past disappointments. Provided that you won't abandon yourself, you can improve the world.

Your Past Isn't A Predictor Of Your Future

If there's one takeaway from all of this, your history doesn't always determine your future. It doesn't matter how many times you've failed before; you can always succeed. Life's greatest significant achievements are rarely simple. Everyone who has succeeded has started with a "want to be."

What differentiated these individuals was their ability to "fail ahead." They learned from their mistakes to avoid repeating them. You might utilize these crucial lessons to reclassify your concentration and drive you to future accomplishments assuming you stay fixed on your objectives and gain from your difficulties.

Continue Your Journey

Positive self-talk may appear to be the only thing keeping you going at times. But, no matter how difficult things get or how little others believe in you, you are in charge of your destiny.

Continuously recall that you are the person who concludes how you will continue and that you should persist. Achievement will come as long as you do not stop doing your best.

Show Gratitude

One of the most desired attitudes is gratitude. You must have a lot to be thankful for. So why not show your appreciation, even to yourself? It is completely free and provides numerous benefits.

Say Something Kind

Saying thank you is the quickest, simplest, and most straightforward method to express gratitude. A few pleasant words will suffice if you don't have something specific to thank someone for. Kind words uttered with sincerity are like a salve to a tortured soul. You will be assisting people who are worried, neglected, sad, exhausted, or somewhat uneasy or discouraged. After all, don't you feel better when someone says something nice to you?

Make Plans That Include Others

You probably know someone lonely or isolated or could benefit from a break from caring for a loved one. What would it take for you to invite that person to join you on an outing, enjoy a coffee or beverage at a local restaurant, see a movie, or take a walk with you? Engaging others in your plans show them that you care about their friendship and appreciate it. It's also a simple way to show your appreciation.

Pay Close Attention

On the off chance that you center so eagerly around what you're going to say straight away, you'll miss the center of what another person is talking about. This is a typical event that can be amended with exertion and experience. It demonstrates that you respect and appreciate them when you stop editing their next comments and listen actively and carefully to the other person, demonstrating through your body language that you're in the moment in their conversation. This is a lesson that we all need to learn.

Bring A Lunch to Share

Meal preparation can feel like a nuisance, especially if you're working and constantly stressed. But, do you know someone who would be ecstatic if you surprised them with a delicious lunch? Maybe a neighbor, coworker, friend, or family member may use a little encouragement, which you can simply provide with a cheap lunch. What a lovely way to express your thanks for everything this person has meant to you.

Pay A Surprise Visit

How many times have you heard others invite you to come to visit them? Pay attention if the statement is genuine. This is a subliminal invitation to spend time with that person. They are requesting your presence. Even if it's just a quick stop on your way home from work, church, or shopping, it shows that you care to consider their prior offer.

Check-in By Email

There's always email if you're too busy to come in person. Send a quick message to let someone know you're thinking about them. To complete the note, add some funny or educational items.

Make A Greeting Call

I enjoy hearing the voice of someone I care about on the phone. It's more personal than an email, but it's no substitute for a face-to-face meeting. A call can be surprisingly rewarding. It's a quick and easy way to say hello, and the recipient will enjoy it. Even if you're short on time, exchanging pleasantries might help you feel better.

Inquire If There Is Anything You Can Do to Help

Many people dislike having to rely on others for assistance. However, with so many items on your to-do list, it's easy to grow overwhelmed. So put yourself in someone else's shoes because we all feel this way. As if there's anything you can do, and make a note of it if your offer is accepted.

CHAPTER SIX

Daily Affirmations

Contrary to popular assumptions, self-affirmation can help you stay motivated, but only if you have strong self-esteem.

Assuming you have low confidence, reminding yourself how amazing you are on and on won't help you since you don't completely accept what you're talking about. Remember that before you begin reciting affirmations at yourself each day.

Choosing a positive self-affirmation from the list below could be a wonderful method to enhance motivation if you've got your head correct and have confidence in yourself and your talents (i.e., self-esteem).

Consider it a menu of choices. Choose a couple each morning as soon as you wake up and speak them out loud or write them down. This will help you start your day off on the right foot.

- **I am prosperous**. I will do all I can to prosper. I will work hard, believe in, and stay positive.
- **I am certain**. I have no doubt that if I try, I will succeed. I am sure that if I make consistent efforts, I will succeed.
- **I am strong**. I am not weak. I am both physically, mentally, and spiritually strong.

- **I am capable** of achieving great things; therefore, I will never stop trying.
- **Every day, I get better and better.** I believe that my efforts in the past are paying off. The little hurdles aren't a sign of my failure; they are a sign of my progress.
- **Right now, I have all I require.** So, therefore, I have to be confident and use what I have wisely.
- **I get up inspired because I know each day is a new opportunity for me to do better than yesterday.** Each day is an opportunity for me to beat my yesterday's record.
- **I am an unstoppable natural force.** Therefore, I will not relent. I will keep pushing, and I will never stop trying.
- I am a living, breathing, motivational example.
- **I am surrounded by plenty.** I do not have to beg or live like I have little because I know plenty. And I can use what I have to help myself and my community prosper.
- I have a positive and motivating influence on anyone I come into contact with.
- **I can inspire others.** Therefore, I will never stop believing in myself and in people.
- I'm overcoming the thoughts that try to make me angry or terrified.
- **Today is a fantastic day.** Therefore, I live it know that I deserve to be happy.
- In my life, I'm turning down the level of negativity while increasing the volume of optimism.
- **I'm completely focused.** Yes, I will never take my gaze away from the prize.
- My hardships don't drive me; all things being equal, my fantasies do.
- I am thankful for everything that I have.
- I am self-sufficient and independent.

- I can be whoever or anything I desire. It doesn't matter if others have tried my step and failed. I am unique and meant to do this and not fail.
- My Past doesn't characterize me; my future drives me. Therefore, I will continue to look forward and not backward.
- I use challenges to push myself to learn and grow. I know I need the tough moments to be stronger, and the tough moments bring the best out of me.
- Today will be an eventful day. Therefore, I go out knowing full well that it will turn out great for me.
- I am attentive and intelligent. I will never lose focus because I can learn from all the good and bad things around me.
- Every day, I am more appreciative. I am appreciative of the good things nature has provided for the people I am surrounded with and me.
- Every day, I improve my health. I will keep doing the right things to ensure I stay healthy.
- Every day, I grow closer to attaining my objectives. Therefore, I will never stop moving forward.
- Amazing changes are occurring in me and my life right now because of the force of my thoughts and words.
- I am continually changing and improving as a person. I understand my progress, and I am aware of myself.
- I'm relinquishing each bad self-uncertainty and dread. I can no longer move with the old baggage, including the doubts I had of myself before.

Conclusion

Living a stress-free and healthy life involves a lot of things, but your mindset and way of life are too important for you to ignore in your journey to a relaxed and peaceful life. Think about it. When stressed, which part of your body bears most of the brunt? It is your mind, of course. Stress begins when you start to give your thoughts about too much baggage to carry – too many sad stories piling up to create past residues for you to carry tomorrow.

So, how do you deal with the baggage that torment, weight, and tire the engine that keeps you going? Prioritize yourself. Doing this gives you the chance to relieve stress and establish a relationship with your body, mind, and spirit. But remember, you cannot achieve this without removing the negative feedback you love giving yourself. Therefore, be yourself without being judgmental and self-critical.

Think about this. When your life begins to slow down, and you've had enough waiting for the weekend magic to surface. What do you do? Beat yourself? Crawl through the stage and force the spectacular things to take their form without really putting in the work? The truth is, you must cease from merely anticipating wonderful occasions to truly living, in the concrete sense, in that paradise built in your mind and around you. Your present is all the heaven you have for now. Cherish it. Live in it. Learn to live in the moments of bliss and begin to feel human again.

Think of yourself as a surfer, gliding through the tides of life; think of yourself riding on the waves and letting the current take you across wonderful memories seasoned with a horizon hanging at the earth's edge. You simply surf the tide of life with a sense of joy and tranquility. Now, your life has become a memory you can compare to a classical painting. You move with ease, steadiness, calm, and gratitude. A veil is lifted, revealing a completely new perspective. This is how you maintain a stress-free lifestyle.

Printed in Great Britain
by Amazon